First published 1980 by
Octopus Books Limited
59 Grosvenor Street
London W1

© 1980 Octopus Books Limited

ISBN 0 7064 1365 2

Produced by Mandarin Publishers Limited
22a Westland Road, Quarry Bay, Hong Kong

Printed in Hong Kong

Educational and Series advisor Felicia Law

PDO 79-446

Doctor Wotsit's Zoo

by
Felicia Law

illustrated by
Esther Rowley

octopus

Doctor Wotsit is busy in his office.
He is working on a large chart.

'I can see streets,' says Ginger, 'and large fields with trees. These squares look like homes. Are you building a town, Doctor Wotsit ?'

Dr Wotsit nods.

'Who lives there?' asks Ginger.

'Animals,' says Doctor Wotsit, peering over his spectacles. 'Animals live here. This is my zoo.'

'Oh,' says Ginger, who is a bit hungry, and he wanders off to buy a triple-decker chocolate ice cream.

When Ginger has finished his ice cream he goes back to Doctor Wotsit's office.

'Since you are so interested, Ginger,' says Doctor Wotsit. 'I will explain why I built my zoo.'

'There are too many people crowding onto this small planet of ours, Ginger. These people want room to build their homes, their roads and cities. The more room the people take, the less it leaves for wild animals.

'Take the Asiatic lion, Ginger. There are probably no more than two hundred of these fine creatures left in the world, if that.

'My zoo will care for the many species of animals who may soon die out, or become extinct. My zoo will try to breed more of these rare animals.'

'As you know, Ginger, I am a doctor of science. And you can be a reasonably useful doctor's assistant. 'We shall work with these animals, you and I, and learn as much as we can about them.'

'For a start, Ginger, you must watch what they eat.

'When you were young what did you eat ?'

'Salami grillburgers, popcorn cereal and knickerbocker glories,' says Ginger.

'Then you are an exception. Most animals learn to eat the food they find around them. If that food becomes scarce the animals may die. But if the animals can be tempted to change their diet, they may be able to survive elsewhere.

'That is another reason for my zoo. You and I are going to study the animals.'

'Pay attention Ginger,' says Doctor Wotsit. 'I sometimes think that your brainpower could be a little sharper. It will do you good to study.'

'I like studying,' says Ginger, 'it's just that I don't seem to learn much.'

'Then I hope you are an exception in this too, for I shall invite all the children to visit the zoo to learn about animals. And the children will teach their parents. My zoo will be an educational centre.'

'Couldn't I just sit around and watch the animals?' asks Ginger, who is beginning to think the zoo sounds like a lot of hard work.

'That,' says Doctor Wotsit, 'is the final purpose of my zoo. It is very pleasant just to stroll amongst the animals, admiring their fine coats and markings, or their strong, muscular movements.'

'My granny likes animals,' says Ginger.

'Then she will enjoy the peace of my zoo,' replies
Doctor Wotsit, 'for I have laid out pleasant walks
through parkland. She will see flowers and lakes. Now,
Ginger, off we go. There is a great deal to be done.'

15

'Here is the Tropical house,' says Doctor Wotsit, 'where everyone will pay a small extra fee. It costs a great deal of money to run a zoo. Of course, all the animals must be fed and well-cared for and that costs money. You cost money, too Ginger, for you are my head assistant.

'Some of the animals have been brought here from much warmer countries. They need specially heated homes.

'The newborn baby animals may need special attention in expensive incubators. When they are fully grown we shall need more cages to house them. We shall need a great deal of money, Ginger, as I believe I have already pointed out.'

'Inside this strong concrete cage are two gorillas, a
male and a female. Sometimes the male gorilla argues
with this wife, so we take him next door to visit his
second wife.

'The gorillas swing on the bars and rings hanging from
the roof. They climb on the tubs and run up and down
the sloping floor.

'In the forests, the gorillas get plenty of exercise as
they search for food.
Here, their food is found for them but they still need
plenty of exercise.'

'This cage is for the chimpanzees. Smaller monkeys are even more active than big ones, Ginger. Be careful of your cap.

'See how they grip the bars and swing along on those long arms. See how they use their tails to swing and give extra balance.'

Ginger wants to go in and play with the chimpanzees.
They seem to have some good toys, balls, bats, rubber
rings, hoops. Ginger can even see a bike.

'Chimpanzees learn very fast for they are extremely
intelligent. They like to copy human beings. I do not
think it would improve them to copy you, Ginger,
although I regret that may sound unkind.'

RUFFED LEMUR
MALAGASY

Africa

LEMUR VARIEGATUS

Doctor Wotsit shows Ginger the label on each cage.

'Here is the name of the species,' he says. 'Here is the country from which it came. This is the special Latin name which tells us about the animal's family. Animals like gorillas and chimpanzees are called primates.'

Doctor Wotsit takes Ginger to see a smaller primate.
    'Ruffed Lemur
    Malagasy
    Lemur Variegatus' he reads.
'Although the lemur lives happily in a big family group, it likes to have somewhere private of its own.'

'I do too', says Ginger. 'Everyone knows which is my room 'cos it has "enter at your peril" painted on it in yellow paint.'

'Luckily the lemur manages without yellow paint,' says Doctor Wotsit. 'See how the male is rubbing his smell along the bough. "This is my territory" he is saying. "This is for me and my mate and our offspring." '

Doctor Wotsit shows Ginger another animal who marks out his territory.

'Many animals do this in the wild and out of habit, they mark their zoo enclosures too.'

Ginger and the Doctor watch the bears. The male trudges solidly round his grassy enclosure. He never puts a paw off his beaten trail, which weaves in a figure of eight through the grass.

'Doesn't he get bored walking round the same path all day?' he asks.

'Sadly, Ginger, you may be right,' observes Doctor Wotsit. 'Animals in zoos are like guests in rich hotels. They do not have to fight or hunt. Everything they need is brought to them.'

'That is why the design of the cage is important. That is also why we take so much trouble finding each animal a mate.

'Do you remember the famous Giant Panda in London zoo ? His name was Chi-Chi and a mate was brought to him all the way from China. But Chi-Chi was not interested and soon the female panda had to make the expensive journey home again. Everyone wanted to see a baby panda for they have never been born to animals in captivity.'

Ginger enjoys seeing the baby animals. Often he can't find them for they stay close to their mothers, hiding in their fur or curled asleep within their paws.

He spies the baby kangaroo peeping out of its mother's pouch.

'So there you are,' says Doctor Wotsit. 'If I had a pouch like that I would put you inside to stop you getting lost.'

'I would enjoy that,' says Ginger happily, 'especially if you have strong back legs and could jump along the ground at such a speed!'

'Time to do some work,' says Doctor Wotsit, and he helps Ginger into a long white overall and an apron. 'Time to feed the seals in the pool.'

Ginger holds the fish high in the air, and the seals hump themselves onto the concrete, blowing and sniffing at the tasty smell. He throws the fish high in the air and they rise on their front flippers and neatly snap in the food.

When the bucket is empty, the seals lose interest. Splash, they shower Ginger with water as they fall clumsily into the pool. Underwater, they loop and glide so gracefully until after a few minutes they rise snorting to the surface for air.

'It will not take you long to feed the pelicans,' says Doctor Wotsit. 'They will take the food for themselves from the bucket if you're not looking.'

The penguins waddled towards him on their webbed feet. They flapped their little wings in protest when Ginger tipped the bucket into the water. Now they had to dive below the surface for their food.

Nearby the pelicans yawned and waited. Ginger threw the fish into those wide gaping mouths with their huge pouches hanging below.

They yawned for a second helping. Ginger yawned too.

'Yawning is catching,' said the Doctor. 'I have brought some sandwiches. Let's sit on the grass and eat our lunch.'

'It is very peaceful here,' says Ginger, as he lazes on the grass. 'Why are there no animals?'

'There are plenty of animals, Ginger, but you haven't noticed them,' says the Doctor.

Ginger hunts all around. Something stripey moves among the slatted shadows of the bushes.

'I think I see a tiger,' says Ginger. 'Yes, I do. No, I don't.'

'The tiger's skin hides him in the jungle shadows,' says the Doctor. 'This is called camouflage.'

Later, Ginger learns of other animals who camouflage against their background.

'I nearly stepped on that snake,' he says in a horrified voice.

'No you didn't,' says the Doctor. 'It is a harmless and timid breed, and it moved away when it heard you coming. But I agree, it did camouflage well against the sandy rocks.

'Look on the wall above your head and see the chameleon. That little creature changes colour depending on where it is resting.'

Ginger drives the meat truck to the lions' enclosure.

'Are we safe?' he asks Doctor Wotsit, 'for there is no wire around the lions.'

'Lions can spring high,' says Doctor Wotsit, 'but they won't leap this dry ditch. The lions like to feel they can roam although they spend much of their time basking under the trees. Throw in the meat, Ginger. The smell has set them prowling up and down in a very angry fashion.'

Ginger learned that all the hunting cats are called carnivores. He threw meat to the jaguars, the leopards, and the cheetahs. The puma would not move from his resting place in the fork of the tree.

'He can't be hungry, Ginger. Unlike you, these animals only eat when they are hungry. In the wild, they may go several days between one hunt and the next.'

Ginger and Doctor Wotsit put on clean white overalls, caps, and plastic gloves. They push open the door of the Quarantine Centre.

'This young raccoon arrived from the forests of North America last week,' says Doctor Wotsit. 'We shall keep it here for several weeks to check its health. Then it can join the other raccoons in the zoo.

'Now pull the mask over your face, young Ginger, because an operation is taking place in the surgery.'

Ginger sees a young ostrich stretched out in the surgery. It lies very still while the vet pulls a plastic cord from its throat.

'Cheer up, Ginger,' says the vet. 'Once the anaesthetic wears off it will feel as right as rain. I hope it has learnt by this dangerous lesson and won't pick up rubbish that's thrown into its cage again.'

Ginger promises to be watchful. He must stop the visitors from feeding the animals with their picnic scraps.

'Why don't they read the signs ?' asks Ginger, who often wonders about people but still doesn't understand.

'They do, Ginger, but they think they know better,' says Doctor Wotsit sadly. He also wonders about people a great deal and he *does* understand.

Ginger helps prepare the feed for the quarantine
animals and all the guests in sick bay.
He chops the fruit and nuts for the marmosets.
He soaks the pellets for the Orang Utan.
He carefully weighs out the food and slips in a vitamin pill.

Ginger stares at the White-tailed sea eagle. The White-tailed sea eagle stares at Ginger.

'You are an ugly brute,' thinks Ginger, 'with your large hooked beak and your strong black claws. I can imagine you swooping down on some poor rabbit with those powerful yellow feet.' The beady eye doesn't waver.

Doctor Wotsit finds Ginger staring into a mirror in his office.

'I have been looking at animals all day,' he says. 'I wonder what they see when they look at me.'

'You are wiser than I thought, Ginger,' says the Doctor, 'for you have learnt that you are just one animal among thousands. Time to go home and rest now,' and he turns out the light.